ACCLAIM FOR ANTHONY VALERIO BY SHEL SILVERSTEIN

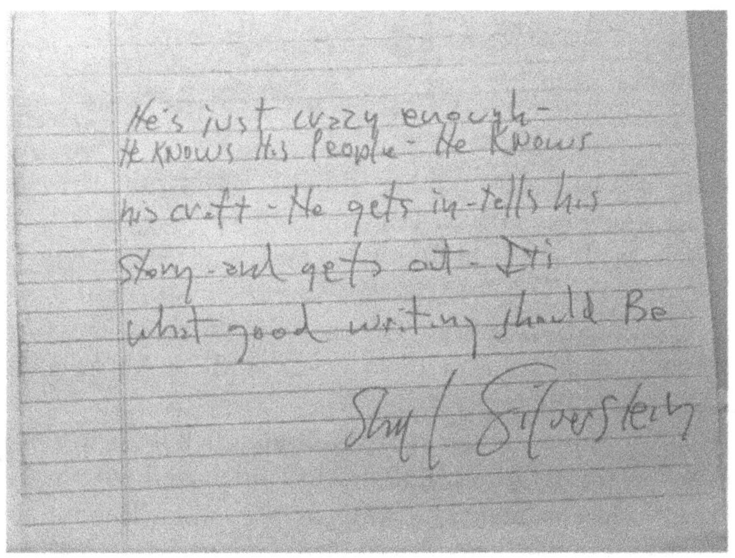
He's just crazy enough—
He knows his people— He knows
his craft— He gets in—tells his
story—and gets out— This
what good writing should Be

Shel Silverstein

Hand-written by Shel, given to the author, 1987

ANTHONY VALERIO

Professional book editor: in-house: McGraw Hill. Freelance: Bantam Books, Grove Press, Popular Library. Fortunate to edit great writers such as Toni Cade Bambara and Shel Silverstein (freelance basis).

Stories: Paris Review. George Plimpton was my first editor Stories anthologized by Random House, William Morrow, Ballantine Books, the Viking Press.

Books: editors included Larry Freundlich who in the mid ‘80s had his own imprint with Scribner. Larry published me with *Valentino & the Great Italians* and *Reaching for the Stars.*(Ballantine Books). Corlies (Cork) Smith--Executive editor Harcourt/Brace *BART: a Life of A. Bartlett Giamatti*; after Cork was fired and freelanced, we worked on the following together: *Anita Garibaldi, a Biography; Toni Cade Bambara's One Sicilian Night, a Memoir* and *Conversation With Johnny, a Novel.*

Teaching: New York University; City University of New York, graduate & undergraduate; Wesleyan University.

Member Authors Guild. Was fiction judge on PEN's Prison Writing Committee.

Illustrated by **Dave Barry--**

Innovative, hands-on, interdisciplinary Art Director & Designer with over a dozen years of experience and a balance of both in-house and agency tales to tell. A visual storyteller who connects brands with meaningful user experience with an eye for detail, innovation and pixel perfection. Having worked for industry leaders including MakerBot Industries, World Wrestling Entertainment and Marvel Comics. I've been extremely fortunate to have had the opportunity to create fearless, original and useful design in most mediums. Recipient of the Hermes Creative Awards for PK Network for exceptional design and development of the NY Cosmos Team Poster.

ALSO BY ANTHONY VALERIO

The Mediterranean Runs Through Brooklyn

Valentino and the Great Italians

BART: a Life of A. Bartlett Giamatti

Conversation with Johnny, a novel

Anita Garibaldi, a Biography

The Little Sailor, a Romantic Thriller

Toni Cade Bambara's One Sicilian Night, a Memoir

John Dante's Inferno, a Playboy's Life

Dante in Love

Immigrants according to Anthony Valerio

Semmelweis

BEFORE THE SIDEWALK ENDED:

A WALK WITH SHEL SILVERSTEIN

ANTHONY VALERIO

a Daisy H. Media Production
a Division of Daisy H. Productions, L.L.C.

FIRST DAISY H. PRODUCTIONS L.L.C. BOOKS EDITION 20/20

Illustrated, with original logos, photos & map by Dave Barry
Cover design & creation©20/20 Dave Barry

Library of Congress Control Number: 2020916405

ISBN: 978-0-9772824-2-5

dedicated to Shel Silverstein - friend & mentor

I hear his voice. See his eyes with brows elevated when he was interested. Miss our conversations.

Acknowledgments

Thanks out to Mitch Myers curator of the Shel Silverstein Archive for his assitance.

Professor Ellen Nerenberg read the mansucript in its stumbling form and offered suggestions that contributed to it being the best it can be.

Grandson Sam expressed interest in Shel years ago which encouraged me to write it in the first place. He may not have known but that's the beauty of having a great grandchild. Thanks also to the Grands Alex, Zoe & Stella for being who they are.

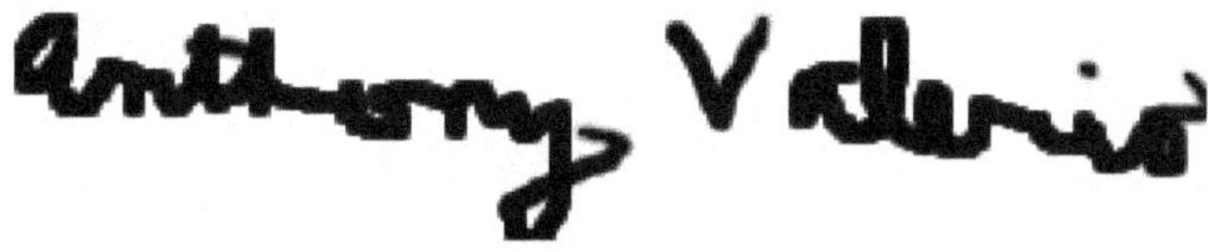

20/20 - Year of the Global Pandemic

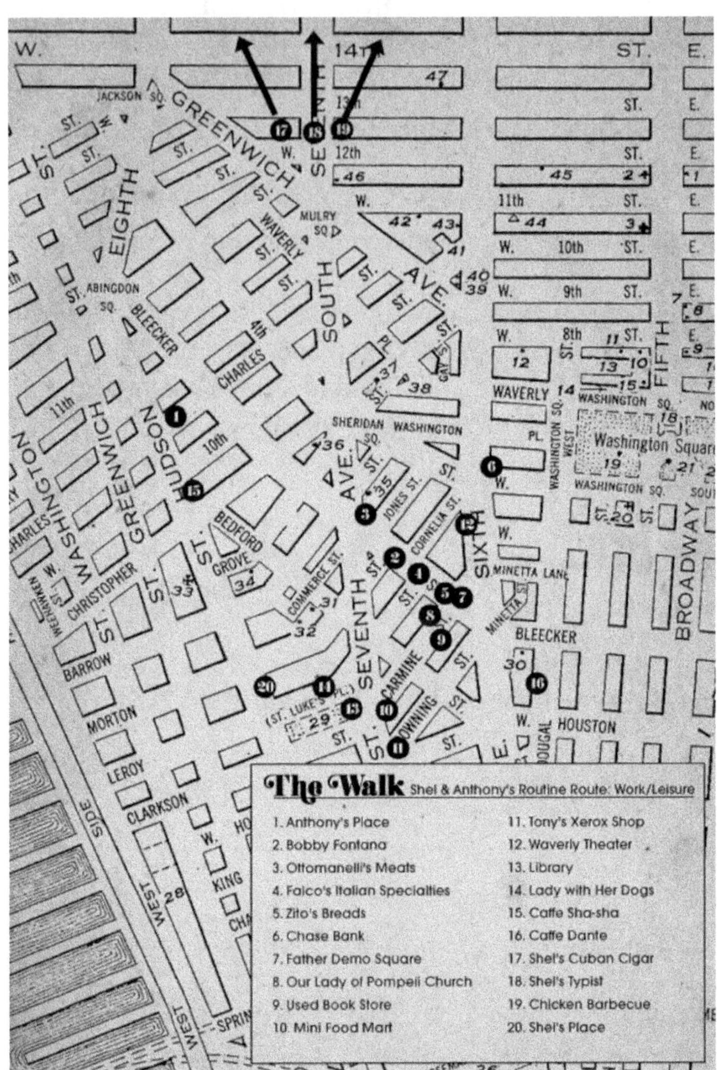
The Walk Shel & Anthony's Routine Route: Work/Leisure
1. Anthony's Place
2. Bobby Fontana
3. Ottomanelli's Meats
4. Falco's Italian Specialties
5. Zito's Breads
6. Chase Bank
7. Father Demo Square
8. Our Lady of Pompeii Church
9. Used Book Store
10. Mini Food Mart
11. Tony's Xerox Shop
12. Waverly Theater
13. Library
14. Lady with Her Dogs
15. Caffe Sha-sha
16. Caffe Dante
17. Shel's Cuban Cigar
18. Shel's Typist
19. Chicken Barbecue
20. Shel's Place

Author's Note

Shel Silverstein passed away on an ordinary Monday in the spring of 1999. The news came over public radio and immediately I called his friend John Dante of their Playboy days. John was down in Longboat Key, Florida. He picked up. Unlike his great friend, John had a cell phone. He didn't wait for a reason.

"I'm driving there now--" in his yellow Isuzu—"He woke up and it hit him. Heart attack. On the way down he hit his head."

Forever etched in memory is Shel getting up in his house on Elizabeth Street in Key West, Florida—on May 10, 1999—suddenly, his chest feels like it's caving in, he clutches his right arm, falls and hits his head.

Of a weekend evening in another springtime long before in Greenwich Village sometimes we passed one another strolling on MacDougal Street, arm-in-arm with our respective ladies. Up around the Caffe Reggio, which introduced the cappuccino, Shel's choice of coffees. Inside hung a Renaissance painting from the school of Great

Italian Caravaggio but we were not interested in the long ago. "In the hopper," as Shel would say. One book done, another on the way. Mutual smiles then move on with our ladies. The next morning, we went to work. He said himself:

"I couldn't dance and so the ladies didn't take to me and then later on when I became popular, I was busy working."

Who knows how many lovers Shel had during his lifetime? Hundreds even thousands, some thinking goes. Must have been that way since he kept quarters along with Hugh Hefner and John Dante in the Playboy Mansion from the 1960s, living there off and on, until the day he died. He lived under the same roof and breathed the same air at any one time with forty of the most beautiful women in the world. Playboy Bunnies. Bunny Mothers. Playmates. Starlets. Models. But the truth is quite different. We were confidantes, Shel and I, and in the way of such matters I can count his lovers, at least the ones he spoke to me about, on the fingers of one hand.

Millions of hearts went out to him that day, among which was that of his great friend Barbra Williams, the one person during my 15-

odd years of friendship with Shel who could arrive at any one of his addresses, unannounced. That evening in late May, I walked down to his apartment on Hudson Street, New York City. Along the way I bought a bouquet of fresh spring flowers at a fruit and vegetable stand, on our behalf, Barbra Williams's and mine, then continued on to his downstairs door, located in an attached building with a gray façade and white trim, beside a candy store. At one corner of the door frame, I gently rested his bouquet.

Forever take that walk. Forever lay flowers at his doorstep.

These are memories of our conversations, our walks side by side up and down Manhattan streets, corners we turned, individuals we encountered by chance, shops we entered, phonograph records we looked at and talked about. Once, while the spaghetti was boiling in Barbra Williams's house in Key West, Toots Thielemans was playing on the radio and Shel walked in, listened a moment then said: "Nobody plays the harmonica like Toots." Another time, Billie Holliday was singing. Nobody sang like Billie Holliday.

Shel and I worked together in the Italian cafés of Greenwich Village only on weekdays. The Italian café owners did not have to tell us in so many words that the weekends were reserved for tourists. Sometimes, when spring turned to early summer and the cherry trees blossomed on our common street, Hudson, and the soft river breeze blew across, we sat outside at the Caffè Sha-Sha under a Cinzano umbrella. We sat side by side on stools at diner counters, on small round tables at the cafes, across from one another at the barbecue chicken place on Sixth Avenue that used to be there. All etched immediately, and endured.

by Dave Barry

"Hi, Anthony. It's Shel Silverstein."

Inimitable raspy voice & open "a's" of the great Chicago native, upbeat and always fresh like he was using his voice for the first time with you. Immediately, his unmistakable visage came into view. Full, close-cut, dark beard, bald as a cue ball. Pervasive feeling of his fame followed close behind. Renowned author of *The Giving Tree*, *Light in the Attic*, *Where the Sidewalk Ends*.

In Key West I accompanied Shel to his recording studio. Moments such as this watching him perform behind glass registered in such a powerful way that very little is remembered. The moment wanted it all to itself. Remaining is a Shel Silverstein I'd not witnessed before. Swift on his feet, in a flash moving behind the recording room's glass and motioning, directing everyone and everything on the other side. And then he plucked and he sang.

The great Italian tenor Luciano Pavarotti whom Shel must have heard over the stereo system in one or another of the Playboy Mansion rooms, the great tenor's voice belting out *Nessun Dorma—Nobody Sleeps*, an apt aria in that celebrated house--Pavarotti said that when he sings, he does not hear his own voice. Perhaps Shel did not hear his own characteristic rasp of a voice but he loved to use it, mainly to hum and sing, and now I hear him humming one of his tunes while strumming his guitar, sitting in a cross-legged position, barefoot, shirt open, where I first saw him in the flesh, on the front porch of his house in Key West. Barbra Williams had just pulled up in her blue Merc and parked out front. I looked out the passenger window and up through the white wooden slats of his porch, and there he was, Shel Silverstein, sitting, strumming, humming. Released left hand on Barbra's bare right knee then opened the car door and hustled up to meet him, hand outstretched.

"Anthony," I said.

He looked back down at the car. Replayed making my way up to him.

"Your New York gait, huh?" he said.

I see Shel walking now in *his* "New York gait." Brisk, straight ahead, one foot advancing directly in front of the other, hands and arms free and swinging, bare toes. Shel liked to wear open-toe leather sandals, and he carried a hand-crafted leather bag over his right shoulder.

He could throw his raspy voice. Growing up in Chicago listening to Russian, Hebrew and Yiddish in addition to English, he aspired to be an artist. He developed a ventriloquist act. Created dummies and threw myriad voices into them. Maybe he could even earn a living working children's birthday parties. He performed with a dummy on his knee at Chicago's Gate of Horn during the late 1950's, early '60's, his great friend John Dante told me but John did not indicate what kind of dummy. A child? An animal? Shel's shy, retiring nature was so deeply ingrained that he could not employ his own voice in creative fashion on behalf of his immediate self. He chose to hear his voice fed back from the dummy on his knee, through its wooden mouth and blinking eyes. As he said, Shel was always working. Sketching, writing. While developing his puppet act he wrote songs. Shel heard America's voices and transformed one of them into a song which blues composer and 12-string guitar player extraordinaire Bob Gibson worked in at the Gate of Horn.

Not only disliked hearing his own voice but Shel also resisted picturing himself in his work. Here is how the reluctant artist made a physical appearance in caricature in his first major commercial success,

23 installments of *Playboy* magazine's travel pieces collected later on in a book entitled *Shel Silverstein Around the World.* While he served his country in the Korean War, in Japan and Korea, he contributed cartoons to the army journal Pacific Stars & Stripes. Another soldier from Chicago, Hugh Hefner, also contributed cartoons to the same magazine. Once both were back home in Chicago, Shel brought a portfolio of his cartoons up to Hefner's office, which was not as yet located in a mansion. Hef, as he was called, had just started up a new men's magazine. Shel left his portfolio of drawings with the secretary. A week passed, two, three. He went back up, and this time Hugh Hefner was there and not only did he buy a few of Shel's sketches but he offered him a job. Travel to the capitals of the world, experience, sketch and write and then send his travel pieces back, and *Playboy* would publish them. No, that was not possible, the artist said at first. His drawings of others, their faces and words, set in their exotic locations would duly represent who the author was. As we shall see, Shel liked to be persuaded. He was Italian that way. He liked to be courted. Hugh Hefner insisted. Include an image of himself in his pieces or no go. The young artist acquiesced. His horizon widened. He threaded his life and work through Tokyo, London, Paris, Moscow,

Spain “where Silverstein Fights a Bull”, Miami, “Silverstein in a Nudist Camp”, Greenwich Village, Hollywood, Mexico. And each travel piece contained a caricature of the author: a curious artist type with narrow waist, angular torso and broad shoulders all together in the shape of a bow, wearing a pair of open-toe leather sandals, sporting a goatee and bald, pad and pen at the ready, looking up. The Fireside book has a Foreward by Hugh M. Hefner and an in-depth Introduction by music journalist Mitch Myers, who curates the Shel Silverstein Archive in Chicago.

“…time for a coffee at the Dante?” Shel continued over my land line, alluding not to the medieval Italian poet, but rather to the Italian café named for the bard, on MacDougal Street between Houston and Bleecker Streets, Greenwich Village, New York City.

“Pick you up in a half hour,” I’d say.

Our apartment buildings were within a stone’s throw of one another’s, his along Hudson Street between Leroy and Morton, mine a walk-up on Charles Street off Hudson. From my place to his was a walk of about ten minutes but I had to allot enough time for a stop at the Chase Manhattan bank on Sixth Avenue. Shel was reluctant not only to use his own voice in an act or portray himself in his writings but also to use banks. Soon upon arrival in town, he relied on friends like me to cash a check, enough to last until the onset of summer. He was a mobile creature with his own private migration patterns. He had managed his life in such a way that he lived in perpetual springtime. November-April: Key West, Florida. May-June: New York City. July-October: houseboat in Sausalito. An occasional November-December: Bangkok, Thailand. "I have to take three planes to get there," he told me. Worth the trouble, for he was less well-known in Thailand and could not be easily recognized from his author jacket photos. And he kept his quarters in the Playboy Mansion throughout the seasons.

"Shel owned trailer parks," Barbra Williams told me.

She did not say where his trailer parks were located nor how many nor why he'd invested in them. Perhaps he invested in trailer parks so that folks who also wished to live in perpetual springtime could climb into their recreational vehicle or mobile home or even their car loaded with camping gear and get on the open road, ride to the warmth and into the sunset, pull into one of Shel's trailer parks, set up a portable tent, light a fire, roast and toast and then, darkness falling, strum and hum a crackling tune under the moon and stars.

Off to Chase Manhattan for Shel's cash. Down the narrow steel staircase with peeling blue walls. Though it was Spring, the hallway was damp and dank. Passing the neighbors' doors kept open was tantamount to passing through their thwarted hopes and dreams of becoming a singer and an actress. Our apartments, Shel's and mine, were a straight, counterclockwise shot but the route to Chase Bank and then over to his place was, instead, clockwise. A brief, pleasant detour. The time it took for Shel to smoke down his Cuban cigar. First thing in the morning, he like to smoke a Romeo y Julieta at his massive wooden desk that overlooked his rear courtyard while looking out, musing. After bounding onto Charles Street, up to Bleecker then east toward Sixth Avenue and Chase Bank.

Bleecker & 7th Ave. South

Despite no bank account at least in New York City, no cell phone and laptop for any length of time, Shel was not exactly a Luddite. His telephone land line in Manhattan had an answering device. He had a land line in his house in Key West. Call the Playboy mansion, ask for Shel Silverstein and Switchboard would forward your message. Shel conducted his spectacular life and work unaided electronically or otherwise. Never once did I see him walk up or down a street with an electronic device in his ear. Sounds of the world around were free to come in. Lively chatter of children going and coming. Voices of America. Vehicles coursing north and south, east and west. Hear children's voices and maybe even the voice of his own dearly departed daughter. I have always thought it a terrible irony that one of history's great writers for children once had a child of his own, a girl, and she passed away at a tender age. Shel gave to those who had helped him with his ailing child and those who remembered.

We lived in an era when love was beautiful, so when Shel confided that he was seeing someone, I felt happy for him and hoped the affair was beautiful and long lasting. From time to time I'd ask him about it as a way of keeping those hopes alive. Walking along, side by side:

"So how is it going with____?"

"That's over. She talked me into buying a computer."

This was Computer Lady, the first of his lovers on the fingers of one hand.

I turned and looked at him. He was really worked up. You could see the veins in his neck swelled up. Here was a living legend who composed immortal stories on ordinary, readily available yellow legal pads, using common black markers and for punctuation one-em dashes, like this—and then a new girlfriend tells him to fuck around with a new-fangled machine. So he goes out and buys the finest computer money could buy. She accompanies him to one of the electronics shops along Fourteenth Street, which at this very moment is still as crowded as any bank or supermarket. In one such shop emitting radiofrequency radiation, she buys for him a top-of-the-line laptop computer and then, once back in his apartment, gets "Shel Silverstein" on line, shows him how to use editing functions, navigate with a cursor, search the World Wide Web for research about any person or thing in all of history. He continued, irate: "OK, so now I have a computer and I use it to reserve a suite at the Plaza. I use it to buy a bouquet of roses. And I use it to reserve a table at the Four Seasons." He was winding up. "But I can't use the computer to fuck her!"

The last time I spoke to Shel Silverstein over the phone was from a Connecticut Super Stop & Shop. I was pushing a loaded shopping cart with open wire sides when I noticed copies of Shel's *Falling Up* in one of those revolving book racks found in pharmacies, airports and supermarkets. High volume places he was reluctant to visit but where his books were displayed. His books were of such high literary quality and widespread appeal that they were mass marketed. Mass market author, intensely private man. If banks begin to display books, Shel's books would be found there. So I took out my cell phone, found his contact phone number and pressed the call icon. He picked up. It must have been my winter and his spring in Key West.

"Hey, I'm in a supermarket in Connecticut and your book *Falling Up* is here and it's doin' good. One copy left!"

The last thing Shel Silverstein needed was an update on sales from a supermarket outlet in Connecticut. Still, my voice was instilled with an artist's enthusiasm, knowing how hard it is to write a good book and then have millions of people read it, generation after generation. Knowing how all of us, including Shel, have had work rejected. Rejection bookended his career. Getting started with his books for children and then, toward the end, getting his plays produced. He was gracious all the same. His voice soft. "Yeah, it's doin' good," he said, adding, "I worked on it for years. Those drawings are some of my best."

Shel did not cook. He juiced, in Key West. After we met on his porch, Barbra Williams joined us and we followed him into his kitchen where he juiced carrots, beets and celery. I did not once smell the aroma of coffee brewing in his apartment or in any one of his homes. I did not once see him carrying groceries. In addition to staying out of banks, he avoided supermarkets. Dial 7 for room service in his suite in the Playboy Mansion. On any given night, he could just as easily have taken his friends to dine at the Folie à Deux in Paris as the Tenth Avenue diner in Chelsea, New York City or a toasted ham & cheese panino at the Caffè Dante on MacDougal Street. I used to go with him to a favorite lunch place on Sixth Avenue. Big black men in white aprons and chef hats smiled out at us, their grilling tongs poking and turning chicken parts on a sizzling charcoal grill, vapors rising. Shel enjoyed his barbecued half chicken with sides of collards, hash browns and warm biscuit with a slab of real butter, costing at that time about $25 for the two of us. Then happily we carried our trays to the small back room, where, I recall over one such chicken fest, he said to me, out of context yet very much in character, "Anthony, has a woman ever told you what she feels when she comes?"

Put down my knife and fork, sit back. “Uh. You mean, ‘-oh-h, honeeey…yes-s there…’ Like that?”

“No, I mean how she feels.”

“Ok, I guess not,” I relent.

“They never do.”

On the south side of Bleecker Street at about its center, meet Bobby Fontana, Watchman of west Greenwich Village.

“Hi Bobby,” and Bobby nods, meaning: “You are familiar, therefore you can pass in a safe manner.” He is disheveled, sour of disposition, deathly pale. For an Italian from Naples whose ancestors worshipped the sun and blue skies and sea and with hearts full of song, this progeny named Fontana was never in the sun nor did he make his way down to the nearby Hudson River. All winter he stayed upstairs in his tenement apartment, awaiting springtime. Then he alighted onto Bleecker Street on one crutch, opened his portable table, set it against his old building’s facade and displayed his wares of packages of men’s underwear, unisex-sunglasses, knock-off pocketbooks. After opening and sitting in a simple folding chair, Bobby watched, conversed and transacted until sundown. He'd seen Shel in my company practically every spring for fifteen years.

"Bobby, say hello to my friend Shel Silverstein. He's a writer."

Bobby shrugs, meaning, so?

"Children's books. He writes books for bambini."

"Ah, for kids," and Bobby squints into Shel's eyes, reining in on his thought just out of range of reconciling some bald guy with a full dark beard with writing books for children who is Anthony's friend. Bobby nods. We are safe. We can proceed.

Up a few shops east toward Sixth Avenue was Faicco's salumeria, an Italian specialty shop, where I'd go for the antipasto and ingredients for the "gourmet" pasta dinner Shel desired. Garlic/imported virgin olive oil/mozzarella in the water made in the rear of the shop/imported provolone/peppers/black olives and mushrooms which I stuff with bits of bacon and breadcrumbs. Type of pasta? Pappardelle con ragù alla Bolognese? Alle vongole (clams)? Puttanesca requires olives, anchovies, capers, oregano? Tending toward pasta alla siciliana: anchovies with their juice from the can, along with chopped black olives, minced garlic added to virgin olive oil, and toasted breadcrumbs. Pasta Siciliano was a favorite at Barbra

Williams's house in Key West, and it was over this particular pasta dish that we gained an insight into Shel's character. He loved to be egged on, especially at table. He grew up during America's Great Depression of the 1930s, and so, after dinner, his appetite may have kept calling. Or, which is what I believe, he loved food and he loved to eat. At Barbra's house we were finishing up first plates of that Sicilian recipe, with plenty left in the serving bowl. You could see and virtually taste hundreds of tantalizing remaining strands of spaghetti. One of us said, mostly likely Barbra, who knew him better than anyone,

"Shel, have a little more."

"I don't think so."

Me: "C'mon, *bis* (another in Italian)."

"Nah…"

Barbra: "Shel, c'mon. You know you want some more."

"Well, O.K.," and he raised his brows and reached across for the serving tongs in the bowl, which he gripped, then one thing leading to another, carried them over and into his plate.

Gossip had it that a few countermen at Faicco's salumeria were gay. The shop was a hop and a skip from Christopher Street, where gay men and women came and walked arm in arm, stopped and kissed, strolled down to a pier jutting into the Hudson River, sat, legs dangling off, and turned their faces up to the sun. Of a late sizzling summer evening, maybe go into one of the abandoned warehouses also jutting into the river and find a lover. We lived in Greenwich Village at the height of the AIDS epidemic of the 1970's and '80s. Faces familiar to myself and Shel: Tommy, Shay, Carlos—dead from that day's pandemic, the H.I.V. virus. We saw mustachioed Carlos off at the airport, on his way to his home country of Chile, to die.

Directly across from Bobby's set-up was Ottomanelli's butcher shop. Inside there were five butchers composed of three generations of Ottomanelli's: grandfather, sons and grandson. All wore bloody white aprons and stood behind a long refrigerator case containing the day's slaughter. They cut, carved and sliced and, at the same time, fulfilled orders. From outside the store window you could see that one line was much longer than the others. At least two generations of Italian women all made up and dressed to the nines were waiting to be served by the young, handsome grandson Ottomanelli. I imagine Shel was with me.

"I mean, Shel, couldn't that young butcher play Paul Newman as a butcher?"

"He could," Shel agrees.

He would soon read in a book of mine about Great Italians about how those women in the butcher shop were like the women who created a matinee idol out of Rudolph Valentino, going to a movie theater and in the dark watch a beautiful Italian lover dance a tango, fight a bull, sweep a damsel in distress off her feet in the desert and bring her back to his tent, bend her back and kiss her like she's never before been kissed. The women in Ottominelli's were waiting to be observed by a handsome, smiling butcher in a bloody white apron across a field of carved up dead animals if only for a brief transient time. While hubby was at work and the kids were in school. Widows. Closer, closer the line gets to him then, smiling, Paul Newman the Butcher says:

"Good morning, how can I help you?"

A few shops further on toward Sixth Avenue was the storied bread store Zito's, owned and operated then by one Charley Zito, who, for the greater part of the 20th Century, knew everything and everyone in west Greenwich Village. There once was a fish store next door to Zito's and one winter afternoon when Shel was not with me and the fish store was boarded up, I mentioned to Charley, "The fish—"

"They got to him last night," Charlie cut it off.

How that incident came about, only Charley knew, most likely from that Italian guy who walked around the Village in a pair of pajamas, bathrobe, slippers and peaked gabardine cap, surrounded by four big men in dark suits and sunglasses, whose families came to Charley's for the day's Italian loaf. Charley's belly rested against his counter, and behind him on the wall hung a large format black and white photo of Charley beside a smiling Frank Sinatra, together holding a giant loaf of Zito's Italian bread. Each and every morning around three a.m., Charley and his family whom none of us ever saw baked the day's bread in ovens in the store's basement. The aroma of warm baking bread wafted up through the steel-slatted grate on the sidewalk just outside his storefront window, out and up into the air above

Bleecker Street, into our open windows and played around our nostrils, Shel's and mine, as we slept, each in our own bed, not far away.

Once you cross Sixth Avenue to the east side you have, temporarily, left the Italians. That might have been the idea of Mr. Chase of Chase Manhattan Bank, for ever since the Great Depression, Italians of the first and many of the second generation use the underside of their mattresses as savings bank. I imagine that "Chase" had his bank's facade built mainly of glass so that its ATM machines, tellers and managers were visible to pedestrians and drivers who just happened to pass by and turn their heads. From the street, everything is visible while inside everything is private. Like Shel's persona. Chase's underground vault of safe-deposit boxes filled with family heirlooms, jewelry, bonds, cash and so forth are kept in steel drawers, much like bodies in a morgue, behind a mammoth reinforced steel door several feet thick the entrance to which only a vault manager has the key. Projecting that in this community of artists and first, second and third-generation Italians, some may be intensely private. Chase in all his wisdom had cubicles built for his managers on the main floor. Square private spaces of three walls and no ceilings with room enough for two, customer and banker. You enter the bank proper, sign in on a computer and wait for your assigned manager to come out, announce your name and lead you back to his or her private cubicle. Or you can wait in a series of white plastic armless chairs. Shel would have a jump start in that I already had a manager, and so it was just a question of whether Mrs. Ahura had room to accept him as a new customer. She recognized my name on the computer sign-in register, which Shel with an appointment and accompanied by me would not have to use. Here's Mrs. Ahura out from her cubicle, smiling out at me.

"Be with you in a moment, Mr. Valerio."

One day while walking side by side, Shel says out of the Mediterranean blue, "Do you know why we like you, Anthony?"

Who were the "we" among the rich and famous whom Shel knew well enough to speak about this Italian from Brooklyn named Anthony Valerio, and then, somehow, these individuals made their way to liking me? I wondered. Maybe Shel dropped a laudatory word or two to his first boss, landlord and great friend Hugh Hefner and sidekick housemate John Dante about how Valerio had written a few good books about Italians and had done a good job editing a book of his, Shel's, called *Three Eyes.* And this Valerio had once been a good boyfriend to Barbra Williams, one of Shel's best friends. It could have been at a Playboy Mansion party and Shel mentioned Valerio in a good light to his friends Dizzy Gillespie, Linda Lovelace, Bill Cosby, Lenny Bruce, Don Adams, Tony Curtis, Momo Giancana, and "Milwaukee" Phil not from Milwaukee. Maybe David Mamet, fellow great Chicagoan and major collaborator of Shel's to whom he sent a copy of my book *Valentino and the Great Italians* for a possible film adaptation, also liked me. It was my experience with the Shel I knew that his inner circle was composed of equally great individuals who hailed from his windy city of Chicago. In addition to Mr. Mamet and housemates Hugh Hefner and John Dante and the Chicago gangsters who visited the Mansion, eminent playwright Herb Gardner. Mr. Gardner was working on a new play about family dynamics destined for Broadway, Shel suggested that he contact Anthony Valerio, believing that an Italian of experience and talent who had written a book that he didn't know what it was but liked all the same, this guy had to know quite a bit about family interrelationships of all stripes. Bob Dylan may also have liked me, otherwise Shel would not have floated the idea to me of writing a biography of Mr. Dylan. In the end, however, I played along and asked: "Ok, why do you all like me?"

"Because you never ask for anything," Shel answered.

Banker Mrs. Ahura issues from her cubicle.

"Mr. Valerio, please come in."

I trail behind.

Mrs. Ahura's customer chair was situated in such a way that Shel would face her open cubicle door but the likelihood was practically nil of other passing customers, consumed by issues of their own finances, turning and looking in. Once I could get him in there, sight unseen, he would not be recognized. He could set up a cash account. His raspy voice being overheard would not necessarily connect him to a famous artist and author of children's books with a full black beard and bald head. Then we would cut out, presto. For some reason known only to her, Mrs. Ahura had told me,

"I'm Italian-American but I married a Palestinian man and we have one daughter."

Then she pointed out to the street, southwestward.

"We live across the street from Chazz Palminteri. The actor."

She was a Villager, prizing freedom and anonymity, simultaneously. You could be Shel Silverstein walking into Chase bank naked as the day he was born—on September 25, 1930—at the prime business noon hour, and nobody would give you a second look.

"Mrs. Ahura," I began, "I would like to withdraw a sizeable amount of cash from my checking account."

"No problem. How much would you like?"

"Five thousand."

"O.K., take this slip to a teller on you way out."

"Thank you. Also, Mrs. Ahura, I have a close friend who is intensely private and needs help in setting up a checking account so that he can also access his cash."

"Is he agoraphobic?" she asks.

"Well…yes, in an odd sort of way. But he's not ill or anything. He just cherishes his privacy."

"I see. Setting up an account wherein he can access his cash should be no problem at all. I do it every day. If you wish, we can pencil in an appointment. Then he can come directly here."

"Can I accompany him? I can wait outside on one of those plastic chairs."

"Absolutely. Just let me open my calendar. Let's see…we have this new-fangled computer system. One day it works, the next….This coming Friday I have a cancellation at 2 pm. That work?"

"Let's pencil it in and if he cannot make it, I will contact you."

"Fine. Name?"

"Sheldon. Middle name Allan."

"Alright, S-h-e-l-d-o-n. A-l-l-a-n. Last name?"

"Mrs. Ahura, do you need his last name now?"

"Well, not exactly now but to open a cash account I will need his full name. He can give it to me when he comes in, or you or he can give it to me any time ahead of his appointment. Now would save us a considerable amount of time."

"Ok. Silverstein."

"O my god! Do you mean, *the* Shel Silverstein!"

"Well—"

"Because I just got *Light in the Attic* for my daughter, Agita. For her thirteenth birthday. It's so refreshing these days with all the independent bookstores closing down to go into a book shop and actually buy a physical book. How wise his publisher is to have that same white cover with black letters and drawings of his. You recognize his brand even before the title. And those author photos on the back jackets! I'll be able to recognize him as soon as he walks in. Agita loved *Light* so much she wants me to get her *The Giving Tree* and *Where the Sidewalk Ends*. Do you think he would autograph a copy for her? I know this is extra, Mr. Valerio, but when Mr. Silverstein comes in, do you think he would mind if Agita stopped by?"

Our Lady of Pompeii Church

With pockets filled with cash for Shel, re-cross Sixth Avenue heading west then cut diagonally across to a street called Carmine, with Our Lady of Pompeii church on the corner. Carmine Street was originally called Carman Street but then first-generation Italians changed it, replacing one vowel “a” with another vowel “i” and adding another vowel “e” to coincide with a popular name for their sons. The whole of this street consists only of two short city blocks, this way there were only so many Italians that could move into the neighborhood.

After surviving steerage class and dehumanizing Ellis Island, immigrants walked from the tip of Manhattan South to Carmine Street and also to nearby Sullivan and Mulberry Streets. Grandfather Don Antonio to Mulberry and Don Vincenzo to a four-floor walk-up on Sullivan above a cheese shop directly across from St. Anthony's church. Don Vincenzo of Palermo and Angelina Rendisi of Avellino met at a church function and their very next functions were to marry and beget six children in rapid succession. Their third child, Gertrude, my mother, sat at the window facing Sullivan Street and gazed across to St. Anthony's church. She mused, "If I have a son, I will name him Anthony." Don Vincenzo was a baritone who may not have heard his own voice but certainly heard those of his hungry children, so, as they were unable to eat notes of an aria, he changed careers to that of a tailor. The more affluent of the neighborhood including local mobsters trudged up those narrow tenement stairs to his apartment, whereupon Don Vincenzo, with straight pins secure in his lips, greeted and began the fitting session by holding up and letting out a few yards of the finest fabric imported from the homeland.

"Heh? Bello, no?" admires Don Vincenzo, holding up a bolt of Vitale wool.

Pajama Don was as reluctant to go up to Don Vincenzo's as Shel was to frequent a bank or a supermarket or, for that matter, a tailor. Throughout the decades I knew him, I did not see him once in a suit jacket or tie. Instead, his fashion could be called "neo-pirate": baggy pants tight at the ankles, long sleeve open shirt knotted at the waist, open-toe leather sandals.

"First one thing then another," says Pajama Don to Don Vincenzo. "Yesterday figlia mi' drags me to shoe store, today to tailor. Next you know shirt and tie maker."

The other Don, Antonio, paternal grandfather—"Here, Shel, is how it works with these Italians….

"Sixteen-year-old Antonio leaves Avellino near Naples because his father Antonio Sr. operated a sheet metal company and groomed his talented son to join him. Naturally, the son grows to hate sheet metal so much that he leaves the country altogether and takes ship bound for America. After stepping onto the tip of Manhattan he walks uptown to Mulberry Street where, in a tenement of railroad-type apartments, one room following another, just like Shel's apartment, Antonio moves in with a cousin named Gus."

S.S.: "Who's Gus?"

A.V.: "Supposedly a cousin. We are all *cugini,* cousins. That's just how the story goes."

"In one semi-dark middle room, under a naked bulb, wearing a white Italian undershirt and worn brown fedora, Antonio Valerio II fashions an adjustable wrench out of pre-stainless steel and this wrench becomes a prototype wrench, along with prototype one-piece knives and shovels, banisters, hospital and insurance company counters and cabinets. Antonio branched out to locks. One of his best customers was Frank Uale, a.k.a. Frankie Yale. No matter how safe grandpa Tony made Mr. Uale feel in his house and social club with no name on the window, he could not do so in his car, especially against the newfangled submachine gun just introduced in Chicago by Mr. John T. Thomson, which, one black night, came to Brooklyn and from a moving car with open window stuck out and sprayed Mr. Yale's car, killing him. Having gangsters as customers did not tarnish Don Antonio's reputation as a fine artisan. It was the time of America's Great Depression, at the beginning of which Sheldon Allan Silverstein was born, and once a week in Brooklyn Don Antonio and the gangsters packed their sedans with boxes of food and delivered them to the poor and hungry. From that time on, as far as their personal well-being and safety were concerned, Antonio and Vincenzo--their families, progeny and friends--were in good hands. Therefore, an Italian with this particular family history residing now in this downtown neighborhood called Greenwich Village pondering, 'Do you know why we like you, Anthony?' thinks but does not say, 'You, Shel, and all your famous friends would be better off down here if, instead of you liking me, that I like you.' "

Father Demo Square

On the corner across the street from Our Lady of Pompeii Church is Father Demo Square, an unexpected, lovely, modest square in the heart of downtown Manhattan where one could sit and muse and rest from speaking with Bobby Fontana and banker Mrs. Ahura and also watch pedestrians hustling in both directions with their New York gait, sometimes Shel Silverstein among them.

"Shel, how is it going with your new lady friend?"

"I broke it off. First it was one thing then another."

This was One-Thing-Then-Another Lady.

I turned and looked at him. He explicated:

"She had a great place in the Knickerbocker Hotel and one night she says, 'Let's go shopping and eat in.' So I go with her to a supermarket nearby…." Not only was Broadway teeming with people but the market was packed with nine-to-fivers. "I pushed a shopping cart while she filled it. She was a big Yankee fan and had got me a cap, she loved the Yankee logo. Then it was, 'Look, Shel, I got box seats to a Yankee game. I love Mickey Mantle! We can take the uptown #2 train at 42nd Street to 168th Street. We'll go early so the train won't be so crowded. I love batting practice….' "

Second-hand bookstore, Carmine Street

Beside a music shop in the center of Carmine Street where Shel felt comfortable enough to stop in and play chords on various guitars stood a second-hand book shop which had a used book stall out front. Shel liked to stop there and browse. Full dark beard bald guy, leather bag over his shoulder, standing at an outdoor wooden stall on Carmine Street, where the sidewalk ended abruptly at Seventh Avenue South.

A mini food mart, larger than a package store but smaller than a supermarket, stood on the southeast corner of Carmine and Seventh Avenue South. Banana Xpress was owned and operated by the nicest

Asian family you would ever want to shop with. The daughter manned the register. "Thank you for coming," she greeted with a smile. The mother and father were off tending to the produce and dairy. Gliding from one section to another, carrying their slow-running hoses from the beans to the carrots to the cauliflower to the sprouts. At checkout, after you paid, Shel with cash, the daughter would say, still smiling, "Hope to see you again."

Seventh Avenue South was the last major thoroughfare before reaching Shel's place. Treacherous pedestrian diagonal crossing against zooming downtown traffic into the narrow mouth of a heavily shaded, snaking block, Leroy Street, which is lined on both sides by majestic London plane trees that did not necessarily originate in London but are planted everywhere in the United States as a reminder of the revolution we had fought to extricate ourselves not only from the capital city of London but from all of Great Britain. These trees were planted a century ago by explorers of the Hudson River who, looking for a respite, anchored at the inlet at the shore, walked up a block or so, liked what they saw and built homes and planted trees within view and sweet salty aroma of the river.

Pass unassuming Leroy Street library where the great Toni Cade Bambara came and sat and read. Then the pedestrian comes to a public swimming pool, in summer kids diving, splashing, screaming. At the chain-link fence beyond the pool, a scene was shot in Martin Scorsese's classic film "Raging Bull," about a sado-masochistic prizefighter, and so how refreshing it is now to come upon an artist's work such as

Shel's that does not include a single imprecation nor episode of violence, unless you count as violent the cutting down of a generous tree. The swimming pool is part of a larger complex bounded on its west side by a baseball field. Across the street on the north side about mid-block lived the ex-wife of a famous film actor. It happened on occasion that just as I was passing, she came out of her front door, her Great Danes not from Denmark but from Germany on either side of her. She was statuesque, skin like honey, drooping eyes that killed, and kept her wide shoulders, head and broad chest raised so high that it appeared that she was advancing to the sky. A magisterial woman stood at the gate to the Shel Silverstein I knew in New York City. Her dogs pranced unleashed on either side of her, equally stately, rhythmically, advancing separate and altogether.

I rang Shel's bell and he buzzed me in and I climbed with a light, brisk step, face skyward. He stood at his door wearing a smile of care and expectation. Sometimes his son and his mother would be visiting and I spoke to them awhile. She was attending university in the Midwest and it was going well. The young lad was doing good, too.

Then Shel and I bounded onto Hudson Street and headed south toward Houston Street and the Caffè Dante. We'd pass the baseball field where a Little League baseball game was often underway, but we did not stop for a look through the chain-link fence. In spring times to come, I'd stop at that fence and watch a game underway and now I picture Shel standing beside, watching. On Houston Street, we'd turn north on MacDougal then walk halfway up to the Caffè Dante.

Houston & Macdougal Streets

Shel was reluctant not only to use supermarkets and banks and include himself in his work but god forbid if he didn't know you and you approached him for an autograph in a public place. I saw it coming out of the corner of my right eye. Rounding the corner of Houston and MacDougal Streets, I glimpsed a young man--mid-twenties, dark hair, short sleeves--across the street, who, after spotting his idol Shel Silverstein, froze, then began running zigzag across opposing lanes of frenetic traffic against the light. Panting, hair blowing over his forehead, wide eyes darting with excitement, he dashed up and stopped directly in front of us, halting our progress.

"O Mr. Silverstein!" I stepped aside. "I don't believe this! You introduced me and all of my friends to such great poetry. Our mothers fell in love with your work, too. I became a poet 'cause of you."

Shel's expression of dead seriousness did not alter, nor had he stirred. Instead, he peered deeply into the young man's eyes. Right there and then, the young man began to recite a poem of Shel's from memory. He attracted attention like he was a street performer. People, total strangers, began to gather around. Cars stopped to watch. Then the young man reached into his cloth backpack and withdrew a slim tome.

"Sir, I'd like you to have this. My first Chapbook. Called *Giving Back.* It's dedicated to you."

He handed it over, waited momentarily for some reaction and then, not getting any, turned and walked away.

In regard to his own salad days, Shel told me, "I write what I want now that I'm rich and I wrote what I wanted when I was poor." That was a time also when he and Quentin Crisp used catsup for their pasta sauce. Crisp was an East Village eccentric character whose signature large, crumpled, black, tilted hat and sharp nose distinguished him even from his good friend's full dark beard and bald head. Perhaps it was better, then, that Shel relied on friends such as myself to make him his "gourmet" dish of pasta. Despite these days of struggle, much like practically all artists, young and old, male and female, known and not so known, here's what Shel Silverstein *did* next on that day. The New York Department of Sanitation maintains trash baskets on most Manhattan street corners, unlidded, open, wire-mesh baskets so you can see the trash dropped in before yours, like the one on the northwest corner of MacDougal and Houston Streets, exactly where we were standing.

"Schwew!" Shel threw the young man's chapbook in there resolutely, with more conviction than I'd ever seen him display. Forcefully, so that it would never happen again. Full motion of his right hand and arm, banging it in there—"Womp!"

Shel was able to enjoy a surge of lightheartedness when focus was shifted away from himself and his fame. One instance occurred under the marquee of the Waverly movie theater, located on Seventh Avenue south, just north of Bleecker Street. It must have been raining and we must have come from Eddie's xerox shop on our way to Shel's Cuban cigar maker and his typist up in the Chelsea neighborhood. Shel and I stood shoulder to shoulder under a movie marquee, gazing out at a spring rain falling in sheets.

A few words about Eddie the Xerox Man. He was an Italo/American fellow who also lived in Greenwich Village. I and perhaps others who used his shop--the only such shop in the West Village then—we used to see Eddie walking around with his wife and baby in a carriage, and we would nod a greeting, "Hi, Eddie," and he would simply nod. He wore always a sad look, forlorn even, in which one could read: "I, too, had ambition to be a writer then I fell in love and married and had a child and, we shall soon see, like your grandfather Don Vincenzo from opera singer to tailor and your publisher from publisher to therapist and Barbra Williams from felon to prosperous executive—I changed careers. On the internet I learned about the great writers in our neighborhood. Allen Ginsberg, Gregory

Corso, Edna St. Vincent Millay who lived in that narrow house on Bedford Street you wonder how she managed and for a time also lived there with a husband, E.E. Cummings, Shel Silverstein, Djuna Barnes, Tennessee Williams. I figured our neighborhood is so charming, you can walk everywhere in a long day, and Bill the Baker was there on Bleecker Street with his French Bakery though Bill was Greek, so more writers would move in. I scrimped and saved, my wife, too, and in time we purchased the lease of that small shop you come to, sometimes alone, sometimes with Shel Silverstein. If you notice, though I have several employees, I myself make copies of his latest hand-written yellow legal sheets that I know some day I will read to my children in a book. Eight cents per xeroxed page up to 200 pages then six cents a page adds up. It allowed me to purchase a nice apartment in the neighborhood. So rather than envy great writers like Shel and yourself, I relish--nay need!--your success so that you will keep coming to my shop. My role is to reproduce, not produce."

Neither of us looked up to the Waverley theater marquee to see what was playing. Rain now was falling in diagonal sheets. Shel was an Italophile first and foremost in his love of Italian cuisine and his attraction to the Mafia for its color and code of silence known as Omertà and its dramatic possibilities and transcendent humor, like Shel himself, witnessed by his penning with fellow Chicagoan and great friend, David Mamet, a film script with the title, "Things Change." Shel said,

"I'm considering asking you to come aboard."

Things Change starred Don Ameche as an everyday guy/mob boss look-a-alike. Every Italian who knows how to make a "gourmet" dish of pasta must also know a little about mob culture. There's a little bit of the gangster in all of us. It's in our DNA. One risk we are born to take is often resembling one another, with our dark hair, eyes and brows, low foreheads, tawny skin. A priest can easily be mistaken for a mobster. Immediately upon receipt of this news of a possible collaboration, I was transported to walking along 57th Street, turned and looked down into a basement barber shop—there was Don Ameche himself, reclined in a barber's chair, a Sanex strip around his neck, his barber in a white gown trimming Ameche's neat upper-lip whiskers. Suddenly, intercepting this reverie under the Waverley theater marquee, a young woman dashed out of the rain, and with raindrops cascading over her shining eyes and full cheeks, approached us. She was holding a book. Oh no, not again! I thought. I stepped aside but she followed *me*.

"Mr. Valerio, I can't believe I recognized you through this pouring rain!"

I glimpsed the red, green and white cover motif of my book *Valentino and the Great Italians* in her hand. She turned the book over to the back-cover author photo. Raindrops from her brow fell upon the snapshot of me standing on my roof wearing a refugee coat and hat. Here's a scan load and post of the original back cover, published in 1987, shortly before Shel and I met.

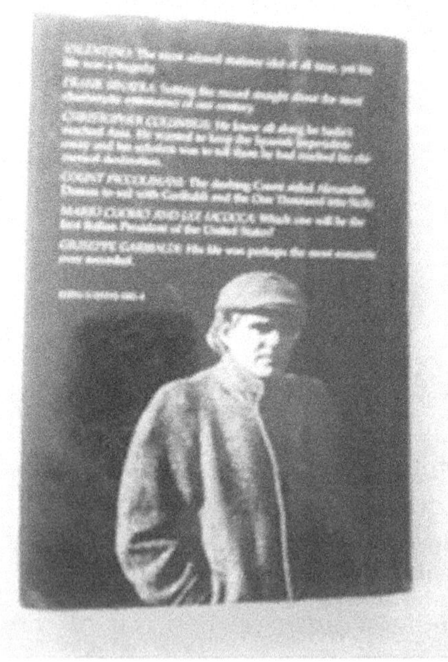

"Forgive the intrusion, Mr. Valerio, on such a dismal day but would you please sign my copy of your book?" She turned and darted a glance over her left shoulder. "It was in the window of the Barnes & Noble up there on Eighth Street."

I, for one, was thrilled. She produced a fountain pen.

"What's your name?"

"Marion," she answered.

"Any special inscription?"

" 'For Marion, Under the Waverley Marquee' and the date—today is, hold on, I have the date on my watch…."

Raindrops on the scrawling ink. After signing and dating and her special inscription, I handed her book back and then smiling, she turned and merged with the other moving open umbrellas. Left standing there, forever. Shel said, smiling:

"I'm impressed, Anthony."

After we left behind the young man who recognized Shel from across the bustling thoroughfare of Houston Street and ran and read from one of his poems, we continued as we did on uneventful days north on MacDougal Street. We passed *Tiro a Segno* restaurant and rifle club. Three flags furled and unfurled in the same line in the river breeze from the Tiro's upper façade. Italy's red, white and green. The Stars and Stripes. The club's own coat-of-arms with insignia of rifles. Here, at one and the same time, you could have one of the finest Italian dinners in New York City, followed by an after-dinner brandy and cigar at the shooting range in the basement. Black tie required down there. Attire of choice at dinner but black tie required in order to shoot your .22 caliber rifle at a sitting duck target while smoking a cigar. It would have been around 11 a.m. on a lovely spring weekday, that refreshing river breeze playing around our faces when we arrived at the Caffè Dante. It had two rows of tables outside but Shel opened the right uptown door, and I followed him into the non-smoking section. We glanced into the freezer case to our right filled with that day's fresh-baked cookies and pastries. We sat at a small, round table, in semi-darkness, against the rear wall. We did not need much of a writing surface. We thought and we discussed. Our wire chair legs, which scraped getting in place against the cement floor, were positioned in such a way that we could both look out onto MacDougal Street. The spring day's arcing sun shone on the traffic, on passersby, and on what each of us perceived in our own way out on the street. One reason Shel liked the Italian cafés was because for sugar they did not use closed mass-produced packets but sugar bowls filled with granules of real cane sugar. Shel liked to dip his finger into the sugar bowl, tick granules off onto his lips, and then, eyes and brows raised, eternal smile of his eyes, we were off and running.

"I don't collaborate with anybody who needs money," he told me.

Liking me because I never asked for anything, including money, and I lived in a small studio apartment out of choice, and was introduced to him by a person he loved, and liked one of my books, he could go ahead and collaborate with Anthony Valerio. He had planned to collaborate on an album of country & western songs with tragic Linda "Deep Throat" Lovelace, whom he'd met in the Playboy Mansion in the early 1970's. More than money, Ms. Lovelace needed help extricating herself from her business manager, who held a gun to her head and, unless she performed certain bestial acts, threatened to kill her sister and her sister's children. That collaboration, however, did not go forward. At the Dante, Shel said:

"Anthony, I'm having a little trouble with a character. This Jewish kid from a Chicago shtetl is gifted with the violin but he wants to be a boxer and his family is dead set against it. I'm stuck right there. What do you think?"

I remembered what he'd said about a woman never telling him how she felt when she came and then a project popped to mind, *Humoresque*--hear the lilting sounds of violin—a film about a similar talented, Jewish, conflicted violinist/boxer, played by John Garfield, née Jacob Julius Garfinkle. Shel was at a new stage in his career. He was searching for a project suitable for his entry into the adult fiction market. I think of saying but do not, "You wouldn't want to venture into the adult fiction market with what's already out there, like *Humoresque*, starring John Garfield." Unless—"Shel, remember that professor of film we heard about, a close friend of John Garfield's, who said that Garfield loved women so much that he had to have several lovers every day, one and then another and another over the span of twenty-four hours? Well, maybe your conflicted Jewish character also loves a variety of women and, for some reason, maybe stemming from an insecurity of his childhood, his life-long quest is to find a lover who will tell him what she feels when she orgasms, but he cannot bring himself to ask, directly, until one night after giving the greatest violin concert of his life to a packed Carnegie Hall, playing Vivaldi's *Four Seasons*, receiving a resounding applause, his tearful, chastened parents in the audience--and then afterwards in a hotel room down here in

Greenwich Village, on a night with the black sky filled with a million stars, while this particular celebratory lady is in throes of physical ecstasy--shivering, seething, bosom heaving, pounding his chest lightly with her fist as if to alert him that she is coming and the time has arrived when it was alright for him to come, too, and he does just that as she is saying, 'Darling, when I come with you, I feel…'– suddenly, in *medias sententia*, as if hit by a bolt of lightning, your protagonist hiccups, catches his breath, rolls his eyes, looks away in search of a final image, then, like a cut down massive London plain tree, falls atop his last lover of the day, of his life."

Maybe Shel's lovers did not tell him how they felt when they came because in their deepest regions, they felt wonderful, and there was no convincing them otherwise, even with their own words, and so there was no need to put them out into the air, into his ears. And maybe he wanted an explication in words that coincided with, or mega-seconds after, her ecstasy. A more civil response, one of a more rounded nature, from a distance that also made sense, something similar to the satisfaction he felt with the dummy on his lap when it was reflecting what the originator, himself, had in mind speaking through a voice other than his own.

Our server approaches. She's wearing a black lace-trimmed pinafore, black apron, straight black hair, black eyes. Professional. Expressionless. Elegant miniature cocktail napkins issued like magic from her dainty half apron. Hovering, pen in hand. Servers then at the Caffè Dante were all women. The coffee and tea makers were men mostly of Hispanic descent, and over the span of thirty-odd years I've not heard them utter a sound. I had occasion once or twice, when alone, to chat with our server. She was from New Jersey, she told me, and had a small daughter and spent most of her time caring for her child and commuting on the Thruway to the café. This kind of incidental information did not come Shel's way because maybe you had to be around in all the seasons, including holidays when most were at home with family. Shel liked his cappuccino. Up to our server, I say:

"Cappuccino and biscotti for me, please. Shel?"

"Cappuccino. Biscotti?" he asks.

She tells him, smiling slightly, "They're like cookies. Shape of a sickle moon. With a little anise in them. I can bring you one to taste."

"No, I don't think so."

I say, "C'mon, Shel, one or two. They're good."

“Well, O.K.”

Back up to her. “So that’s two cappuccini and a double order of biscotti.”

As soon as she turned to place our order, I took his cash out of my pocket and handed it to him. He handed me his check for the same amount. We glanced back out to the street.

“Oh, Shel, I spoke to my banker, Mrs. Ahura. A nice Italo-American woman married to an Arab and they have a daughter. She said she’d see you in her cubicle and open a cash account for you. The cubicle has three sides and no ceiling. Totally private. This coming Friday afternoon, after we work. Ok? I’ll go with you.”

Pause.

“I’ll think about it,” he says.

“O.K. Also, there’s a very good food mart much smaller than a supermarket and a little larger than a package store where Carmine Street ends. A hop and a skip from here and virtually around the corner from your place. It’s run by a very nice Asian family, daughter on the register always smiling, father and mother running a slow hose on the produce, keeping them moist and fresh. Glad to go together.”

Another pause.

“I’ll think about it.”

Hanging on the wall beside our small oval table was a life-size photo of Florence’s *Ponte Vecchio*, the old bridge. Shel said,

“I have a friend John Dante who wants to end his days there, in Florence. Thing is, he’s never been.”

“He should visit first, see if he likes it. No?”

“That’s what I tell him.”

“I think we can work something out along those lines,” I offered. “We can take him to Florence.”

Shel continued: “John’s writing a book about his life in Playboy. He says he’ll use the royalties to move to Florence. Guess what he wants to write about?”

“Um-m--”

“I mean, here’s a talented restauranteur who opened the finest supper club I’ve ever been in, The Touch Club--" John hated dances like the Twist where people danced away from one another, he loved dances where couple touched, hand in hand, arm around waist. Bodies touching. Shel didn’t dance so he did not touch and was not touched, dancing. “John hired the best chef on the west coast, Noel

Cunningham, and Lucille Ball and Michael Caine came and Michael Jackson came and danced."

Friends Shel & John at John's Touch Club, Beverly Hills, 1990's. (courtesy John Dante private photo collection given to the author.)

"And here's a guy," Shel went on, "who hired Bunnies for the clubs. Trained Bunny Mothers. Outfitted the Playboy jet with the Jet Bunnies, the crème de la crème of Bunnydom. Had a hand in starting up the orgies of Orgy Night. And what does J--a--h-n want to write about? Fucking his substitute grammar school teacher."

"I can understand," I actually said.

“Anthony,” Shel went on, “will you help John write his book? He’s living in a hellhole in Fort Lauderdale. Just go down and sit around and talk. Here’s enough money for a week in a nice hotel.”

He peeled off a plethora of hundreds from his newly acquired cache of cash.

“Sorry, Shel. You know I don’t do things like that,” and pushed away his money.

But he did not relent. Time and again at our sessions at the Caffès Dante and Sha-Sha, he asked if I would help his friend John Dante write his book. It was so uncharacteristic of Shel to ask for anything that his appeal made a deep impression. He was returning the way he liked to be cajoled. He was human. He cared deeply for his friend. He figured John Dante and I were a good fit. Née Giovanni Aimola in south Italy, both John and I were Italian, loved food, music and women. A few of Shel Silverstein’s inner circle consisted of reformed criminals, Barbra Williams and John Dante. Before John became a talented restauranteur, he ran a fencing operation in Cicero, Illinois, buying stolen silk suits and then selling them out of the trunk of his powder blue Cadillac convertible. Barbra Williams had once been a smuggler—cash? diamonds?—with a partner disguised as a holy man. Priest with a white collar, holding a hollowed-out catechism, filled with contraband diamonds from South Africa? Or a rabbi with sideburns and blue satin yarmulke, holding his holy, hollowed-out book? What good American customs officer would search a clergyman's sutra? Well, the partners in crime encountered one at a U.S. airport. Their turn on the customs line arrived. Something just wasn't right. A ravishing beauty beside a portly holy man.

"Ma'am, go through, please. Uh, sir, open your bags." The holy man complies. "Ah," says the customs officer, "a sutra. Huh, I don't follow any organized religion but like to say I'm a spiritual person."

That was it. Contraband dope/cash/diamonds in the book hollowed of scripture. Both were handcuffed, arrested and transported to prison. Barbra Williams went on to pay her debt to society. Then she set up a nice place in Key West, took a job selling tourist fare, wrote a book about her transformation from good girl gone rogue then back to a productive life, and sent her manuscript to the reputable New York publisher, Max Zazlovsky.

As for friend Anthony Valerio's criminal ways, through his Dons, Vincenzo and Antonio, some crime had to course through his veins. Also--"How is the teaching going?" Shel would ask as frequently as I asked after his latest girlfriend, knowing that I would not become a millionaire through my books but with teaching at the university I would at least have a roof over my head and once in a while a plate of pasta without catchup. “The teaching’s going o.k.,” I’d say and not go on to talk about my millionaire student who came to class in high heels and chinchilla fur coat, all made up. One night after the course had ended, she invited me to her midtown penthouse. Her husband was there with a group of friends. I recall it as vividly as I can recall a recurring nightmare. I was sitting on a soft cushioned antique couch, surrounded by a group of men I did not know, one of whom says, “We are offering you one million dollars in unmarked bills to smuggle diamonds into the United States from South Africa. In the satchel there beside the couch is five hundred thousand dollars in unmarked bills and then five hundred thousand upon your delivery of the diamonds. As well as a first-class round-trip ticket J.F.K-Johannesburg/Johannesburg-J.F.K. You will be notified of the drop after you clear customs. This is the last time you will see any of us.”

“Shel,” I would have told him, “here’s exactly how I felt at that moment. Profoundly insulted, the persona of a good-looking ‘Tony’ from Brooklyn with tawny skin superseded a published author and university professor. Second, they were out to capitalize on my friendship with my former student, a beautiful woman, and good, too, whom I truly liked. Three, she allowed the offer/insult to occur because she was an abused woman and they had some sort of leverage over her. Abuse of her teacher and friend was another instance of their abuse of her. Which turned out to be the case. Here's what I did. I picked myself up from the couch, bid her good night and left.

Great friends Shel & John (courtesy John Dante private photo collection given to the author)

Shel was the kind of friend like family to whom I could never say no. In the end, I acceded to his wishes and went down to his friend John Dante's hellhole in Fort Lauderdale and helped him with his memoir of his life and adventures in Playboy. We sat around and talked, like Shel wanted. In the chorus of his song "I Hear America Singing," Shel wrote about a lonesome cowboy playing and singing about women with cheating hearts. As long as I knew him, Shel did not live with a woman for any length of time. He lived under the same roof and breathed the same air as women in the Playboy Mansion but never with any single one of them. Maybe he felt lonely. Maybe he pictured himself living with one or more of the women he told me about and came up short of the reality. In the end, I feel Shel was the only true source of this issue. John Dante provided at least some insight. John told me,

"I asked Shel once, 'You know, the life you and I lived"--that is, decades of experience living alongside the women who also lived in the Playboy Mansion—"we learned a lot from it. We know too much about women. We're almost cynical—" Meaning, perhaps, all women wanted from a man was the means to get ahead. They loved you until another man came along who offered a further step upward. Yet, if Shel cared for you, loved you, he was willing to share and give everything he had, all that he knew. Maybe, though, not all of his time. As he said himself, "…when I became popular, I was busy working." Time. He could not give all of his time. The time of his working and maybe he felt he was working even when he was not ostensibly sitting at his old massive desk sketching and writing. Maybe he was working while smoking his Cuban cigar and looking out his rear window, musing. John Dante continued: "If you—" Shel, that is-–"had to do it all over again, would you do it exactly the same way?" Shel answered, 'Without a doubt.'"

John Dante, who originated Orgy Night at the Mansion, also told me—

"Shel did not take part in orgies in Chicago. Maybe once, in Los Angeles."

And John shed some light onto Shel's intense sense of privacy. Even with his closest friends "Shel was always secretive. If we were playing a game in the [Mansion] dining room, we could see Shel pass by with a girl. He'd walk by very quietly. We'd laugh about it."

I wondered throughout the John Dante project why Shel had been so intent on me helping his friend with his book. As a rule, he, like me, never asked for anything. What stake did he have in John Dante writing, publishing and succeeding with his memoir? It could not have been to spend his waning days in Florence, city of other Great

Italians such as Leonardo da Vinci, Michelangelo and Dante. But then after Shel and John died within a few years of one another, one in Key West, the other in Long Boat Key, and I was writing the book Shel had asked me to help John with, and John's life in Playboy was unfolding as was Shel's part in it as his, John's, closest friend, I hit upon a plausible reason. A profoundly personal one, on Shel's part, that is. Historical in nature, his own, Sheldon Allan Silverstein's. A reason that was a matter of his great heart. One that had to do with the young Sheldon Allan Silverstein who could not dance and so was not a favorite with girls and was not good at baseball. After the success of Shel's travel pieces published in *Playboy* magazine, he and Mr. Hefner became friends and Hefner invited him to move into his magnificent home/office/leisure space called the Playboy Mansion. Then Hef invited John Dante to move in. John had owned and operated the fancy after-hours club on Rush Street called John Dante's Inferno. John loved Gustav Dore's illustrations of Dante's Inferno and decorated his stylish club with blown-up photos of those illustrations so that all who came in and sat and looked around saw the levels of hell they could descend to. It became a populate after hours club. Hugh Hefner came and left a few copies of his new magazine. Lenny Bruce came and Don Adams and

Shel Silverstein and other young artists and entrepreneurs. They listened to the wonderful Frank D'Rone sing and play his guitar and Nat "King" Cole play on the old spinet. Ella Fitzgerald came in and sang a few songs. About the possible reason Shel felt indebted to John Dante, John wrote: "Actually, my moving in [to the Mansion] benefitted him because when I went out and did my Bunny Hunts, I brought back some great-looking chics he was privy to, that he got to…."

Maybe Shel was forever grateful because John Dante had given him something that once it passes can never be retrieved. Time. Time for his, Shel's, wit, his humor, his generosity, his capacity to love--all to shine through. Time, finally, for a woman to love him.

"My accountant says I have to spend a few thousand dollars a day," Shel told me, and so on our work day stops in addition to coffees and pastries and lunches, his cigar maker and his typist, we'd go to the basement antique shop located on King Street, which was a short walk from our caffes. Shel and I, two artists in a China shop. When he purchased an item, often a garden sculpture and a few days later he shipped it, soon like a feat of magic that objet d'art purchased in a semi-dark basement in New York City—voila! appeared in his backyard in Key West. Amid lush shrubs and swaying palm trees that for me was paradise, I'd crane around and breathe a deep breadth of contentment. Oh to be alive!

"I don't like my editor," Shel told me in his backyard, guitar across his chest. Barbra Williams was there. She was always there. Her presence is tied to Shel at every turn. It turned out he was talking not about his children's books' editor, one of the most successful in publishing history, but the editor of a new work.

"I'd like to try the adult fiction market with this one," he continued. "It's called *Three Eyes.* Would you take a look at it?"

Barbra must have given him a copy of my new book entitled *Valentino and the Great Italians* and, though he liked it but did not know what it was, he knew what his book *Three Eye*s was and he loved and respected Barbra and through her, me.

"I'm willing to pay you," Shel followed up, and with that withdrew his check book and black magic marker.

Here was an intensely private man, one who avoided crowds at all costs, was reticent to enter a bank, supermarket and goddess knows what other crowded space, yet was willing to entrust his latest masterpiece to a relative stranger.

"I will look at it but not for pay. I do not take money from friends," I said.

I lie with Barbra Williams in her loft bed, a skylight a few feet above us. Reach up and touch the night and the stars. Afterwards, I told her what I felt. She listened then said,

"I told you."

Anthony's Place

Shel climbs the stairwell of my place past blue peeling walls and the still open doors of the lapsed singer and actress, inside yet invisible, ghosts of their once hopeful selves. He enters into my kitchen where I will prepare his "gourmet" dish of pasta. It had a pre-war stove just like in Gertrude's kitchen and a fridge built for use by elves. He takes a few steps and sits in the yellow club chair beside my land line in my combination living room/bedroom/office. Located in the rear of the building, the sole sounds that reached back there were the coo-coos of doves and the staccato horn blasts of a distant train. At his right was an exposed brick wall, some bricks chipped, and the cement binding the bricks had eroded over the decades. On a bookshelf sailed a miniature, twin-masted sailing vessel, replete with sails in the form of seashells, and over the adventures of those same decades the ropes had pulled loose from many a gale, but the seashell sails held.

©Anthony Valerio 20/20

Shel looked out my right window to the majestic Twin Towers and a small scalloped bowl on the ledge where sparrows and doves perched and drank. Then he looked around and, taking in my entire place with one glance, said: "I guess you can choose to live here."

From his shoulder bag he withdrew a Manila envelope originally manufactured from a tough species of banana in Manila and from inside took out typed pages of *Three Eyes* attached to a separate sheet of paper.

"I'd like you to sign this," he said. "It's a non-disclosure agreement."

He had entrusted someone he hardly knew with manuscript pages of a new book and then sought to silence him about it. His brand was worthy of intense protection, his words, his art work and the look of his book covers, white with black topography and signature drawings.

"Of course....Let's see, where do I sign?" I said.

Immediately, whatever memory I would have of my work on *Three Eyes* was erased. The Italian omertà was unleashed, pre-amnesia. *Three Eyes* would exist only for the time I worked on it, which turned out to be a period of months on the open card table in my studio and on a fold-out table in the jet flying down to see Barbra Williams. As the affair with Barbra continued on, it appeared that Muammar Gaddafi was content not blowing up U.S. domestic jet liners. Or, for the sake of love, I took my chances One of the reasons Shel loved Italians was because he knew we are sworn to secrecy even before we know the secret's content.

In general, *Three Eyes* was about a regular guy with an extra third eye in the center of his forehead. While his author was reluctant to be in crowded places, this odd dummy of a protagonist sought them out, yet was puzzled by the quizzical way people around were always looking at him. Mr. Three Eyes felt normal. Maybe for him, everyone else also had a third eye. I can still see this darkly comedic character in a ballpark, looking around quizzically at the people in the stands nearby staring at him. The overriding editor's query—mine, that is--was possible fleshing out of scenes. One example not in *Three Eyes*: In a crowded bank with newly published books stacked in a rotating book rack, Mr. Three Eyes notices a reprint of Euripides' "Cyclops." Other banking customers notice him browsing through the book and rush over for a close-up of his face with a third eye.

Walking side by side from Eddie's Xerox where Eddie made facsimiles of *Three Eyes*, Shel and I passed the Waverley theater then continued north to the neighborhood of Chelsea, located north and east of Greenwich Village. Chelsea is like a shoulder of the Village on which entrepreneurs piled art galleries, cafés and restaurants. Shel stopped at an apartment building, and we went in. He had not announced this stop so maybe he wanted it to be a nice surprise, which it was. The elevator let us out to an opened apartment door behind which stood a short, smiling, middle-aged man with a neat mustache, smoking a cigar. He was Shel's personal Cuban cigar maker. We shook hands and then Shel said something and his cigar maker turned and disappeared in his stacks, which were like stacks in a library only instead of books were endless rows piled with boxes of hand-rolled cigars.

Odd it was to find a commercial shop inside a residential building in a residential neighborhood. Why? I continue to wonder. It was entirely possible that this cigar maker's business was not commercial in the broad sense, it was confined to one customer, Shel, just as his literary agent had one client, a singular customer fortunate enough to afford the best Cuban cigars an American could buy on a steady basis and have them shipped to his other addresses when he was not in town.

We continued uptown to his typist's. Up wide brownstone steps to a parlor floor-through. His personal typist had a shrill voice which she used the entire time her sole client handed her fresh pages to the time we left. From her place we walked up to the Tenth Avenue Diner. We sat on stools at the counter, side by side. We ate quietly, pleased to be in a good diner, then outside we hailed and then waited for a taxi to pull up and transport Shel north to Columbia University.

"I wait for her in the library," he'd told me.

This was his Academic Lady.

Picture Shel lowering himself into a yellow taxi cab, left arm pulling the door closed, and there he goes, pulling away, the back of his head visible as far as a block or so away. A short taxi cab ride from the Tenth Avenue Diner to Columbia University's Low Library. Uptown to Riverside Drive then east to Broadway and 116th Street. He could not have walked unnoticed up Columbia's College Walk, which traverses the heart of the campus. He'd be in the midst of hordes of students who, at any one given time, had been raised on his poetry and drawings, and they would recognize him from his book jacket covers. But, I knew, there was an out-of-the-way staircase that led to Low Library.

"It's on Broadway," I told him, "after you pass the basement recreation room. A set of steps takes you to Low Library's side door."

A professoressa, I thought, might be a good fit for him. She would not be impressed by his fame, and would not be competitive, writing books herself but with a limited audience. She earned enough for decent housing and sustenance. A brilliant mind she would own, unleashing her body in moments of physical pleasure. She could tell him how she felt.

"How is it going, the library…?" I asked him.

"That's over," he answered. And that was all.

His affairs illumine one of mine. I'd been a student at Columbia and a blues singer from Tampa who sang with Buddy Rich's traveling band lived across our common wall against which I heard her body banging often toward the end of the night. Soft pleasant chords from Rich's keyboard player wafted across. Near the ceiling on a shelf around her room stood bottles of urine her lover had placed up there. She threw him out and from time to time invited me in. Our common wall was still of a piece. Late on Sunday evenings, a few band members congregated and they told me, “Go sit at the drum kit by the window and play the brushes.”

She sat against her bed’s headboard, legs up, private parts in plain view. Later on, her screams filtered out her window, into the Broadway night.

We were passing the Caffè Sha-Sha and I turned and said,

“Oh, Shel, would you come with me to the River Hotel up Christopher Street? I rented a suite for the weekend. Barbra Williams is coming up. I’d like to see how it is.”

I wanted him to know I was treating his close friend in a special way.

We passed storefront windows with memorial photos of the men in our neighborhood who had died of A.I.D.S. There was Shay, Tommy, Carlos, whom we accompanied to the airport on his way back home. The hotel was located at the end of Christopher Street, squat on the Hudson River. It had a roof deck that afforded a great view of the river and the sunset. Have a pre-dinner Prosecco up there, faces brushed by the soft breezes. Watch ocean liners towed on their way out, on their way in. The hotel was subsequently converted to a home for A.I.D.S patients. Before these young, beautiful men captured in storefront window snapshots had died, they spent a few days in a nice place. While we were walking, I asked Shel,

“Would you write a few words about my new book?”

Without breaking stride, and without uttering a word, he reached back to his shoulder bag, withdrew a yellow legal pad and from his pants a black marker and wrote the following:

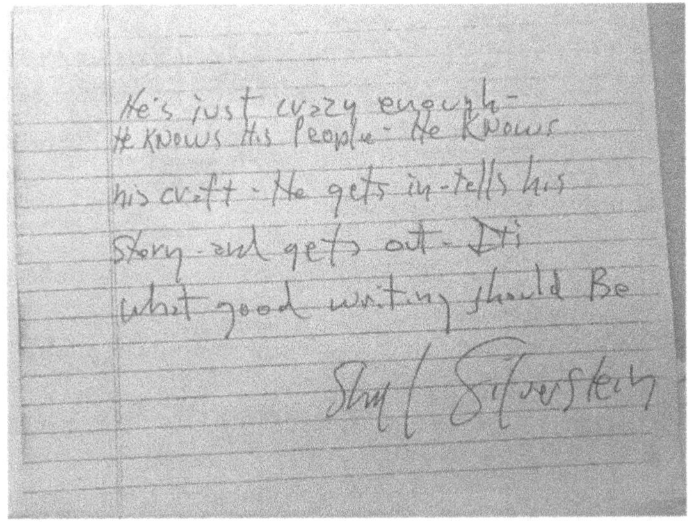
He's just crazy enough–
He Knows His People– He Knows
his craft– He gets in–tells his
Story and gets out– It's
what good writing should Be
Shel Silverstein

As far as Shel Silverstein was concerned, I was “just crazy enough.” Not over the line of the restraint required in this business of creation. “Just crazy enough” to transform reality into something beautiful. The voice of a puppet not quite that of the mad puppeteer. "Just crazy enough" to begin a romance with a beautiful, once felonious woman.

"He knows his characters," Shel wrote.

I knew this character Shel Silverstein well enough to create a literary puppet of him, with full black beard and bald, smart and generous, and throw a rasp of a voice into him with the open "a's" of a Chicago native. This puppet voice says:

"O how I wish he could have gone to Gertrude's Kitchen in Brooklyn and stand beside her and look down at her elegant work-shorn hands stuffing her peppers with breadcrumbs, bacon bits and capers. Rolling, cutting and folding her gnocchi and ravioli and filling them with ricotta. Baking her flaky crust then filling with escarole."

Shel Silverstein is the star. I am its dust.

Here is an example of what he liked but did not know what it was in my book the Great Italians. A work that led directly to our meeting for the first time.

Young Shel loved baseball. He was a fan of his hometown team, the Chicago White Sox. He learned soon enough in the street with a few other boys that he was not good at playing baseball. His thoughts about his sports prowess led him to say,

"When I was a kid—12 to 14, I'd much rather have been a good baseball player…but I couldn't play ball…."

Like most of the other kids, especially those of the Jewish culture, he heard about the Black Sox scandal of the 1919 World Series between the Chicago White Sox and the Cincinnati Reds. It centered around eight key White Sox players who were paid cash for booting routine ground balls, making errant throws from the outfield, pitching fast balls down the middle on 3-balls and 2-strike counts. The fix was engineered by a Jewish gangster from New York, Arnold Rothstein. Boys of Chicago learned that there was crime in the world, gangsters of all stripes, fixes, deceit, people who would sacrifice dignity for money. But the fact that he was not good enough to play did not hold young Silverstein back from witnessing and enjoying the game. Rather than become a mascot or water boy, he took a job selling hot dogs in Chicago's Comiskey Park. At one and the same time, he could earn a few cash dollars and see Luke Appling play a sparkling shortstop, Tony

Cuccinello hit line drives up the alleys. Picture teenage Sheldon Allan, clean shaven and with hair, preparing to go off to the ballpark. Make sure you bring your cash change, $50 in ones, fives and tens. With a black marker write down the access code to where the assignment coordinator was located. He went down there. He steps up. The coordinator:

"Silverstein, beer or franks?"

"Franks, sir."

"All right. Upper deck, son, between home plate and right field."

Off to commissary and the hot dogs, 25 at a time, steamy and juicy, along with mustard and napkins, in a smoking 25-pound vendor box with straps. Strap it on and then up, up to the upper deck, look down and voila! unfolding before your young eyes is, as the Great Italian Bart Giamatti called it, "the Green Fields of the Mind."

"Hot Dogs Heeah!" at the top of the boy's raspy voice.

He earned a commission of 50 cents per hot dog sold, bringing back home a crisp twenty-dollar bill during those dog days of boyhood summers, back in Chicago of the early 1940's.

From the essay on Great Italian “Joe DiMaggio” from the book *Valentino & the Great Italians:*

…Joe DiMaggio was wearing a blue suit the night he met Marilyn Monroe. Mickey Rooney was in the restaurant and when he saw Joe DiMaggio he rushed over to the table and said to Marilyn Monroe: “Do you know who this is?”

“I’m sorry,” she said, “but I don’t know about baseball.”

Mickey Rooney said, “This is the greatest ballplayer who ever lived. Lifetime barring average, .325. 131 triples. 361 homers. 9 World Championships.”

Later on, Joe said to Marilyn, “Don’t feel bad I don’t much about movies.” Then he said, “Would you like to come up to my suite and see my trophies?”

“Are you kiddin’?” she said.

Joe leaned over and kissed her.

April turned to May, the month in which Shel Silverstein died and Anthony Valerio was born and Shel arrived in town. After I’d written about twenty Great Italians, I sought a publisher. Maximilian Zazlofsky, or, as he was called in high school, simply Zaz, went on to become a publishing wunderkind. He had an imprint with the publisher of Ernest Hemingway. If the great Hemingway were alive, I would attempt to persuade him to write a few words about Max Zaz. Brooklyn product, gained fame in the world of publishing, impeccable taste in ideas, books, writers, cuisines of the world. Once a Genius on Vodka.

Max and I were both from Brooklyn and fans of the Brooklyn Dodgers who after they left for California transformed to the New York Mets. I put in a call to him. He picked up right away.

"Before anything else, Tony, I want to thank you for being such a good catcher. No one else could have caught my rising fastball and curveball in the dirt."

Shel did not call me Tony. He called me, always, Anthony.

"Well," I responded to Zaz, "we had a good team. You know, you were a good pitcher. I can still see your full windup. Yes, and that rising fast ball of yours and curve ball in the dirt."

I did not tell him that I was not his catcher, I was his third baseman. Better not bemuse until a later time, if at all.

"Eleven o'clock tomorrow O.K.? Lex Tavern?" Max offered.

"Night-time is just fine," I agreed. "I'm a morning writer."

"No. I mean, eleven in the morning."

"O.K. Eleven at the Lex."

The Lex Tavern was located north and east of Greenwich Village, and I walked there, slowly. It was a way of carrying a bit of that famous place with me. Its history of artists who lived and created there. John Lennon a few blocks north on Bank Street. Janis Joplin around the corner on West 10th. Imagine a Joplin & Lennon duet. Jimi Hendrix two blocks north on Twelfth. Shel Silverstein in a second-story apartment on Hudson Street. In the Lex Tavern, Zaz had gotten a head start. Take a stool beside his.

Bartender: "What can I get you, Tony?'

"Cup of American coffee, please."

Zaz says, "Tony, if you had to choose the best Italo-American catcher in history, would it be Yogi Berra or Roy Campanella?"

Mike Piazza was not yet catching for the Mets.

"Let me think about it. In the meantime, Zaz, I brought along a few manuscript pages."

From a Manilla envelope withdrew the essay titled "Joe DiMaggio". Zaz made room in front of him, set the pages beside a glass of Vodka, and began reading.

In a situation like this, writers can pretend they are not about to die. Zaz turned over one page then another. Pretend not to be watching his every move. Vodka running down. Right hand turns over penultimate page. My coffee regurgitating. Turns to the last page. Cannot breathe. Then his pitching arm reaches into his left inside jacket pocket and withdraws a checkbook. The sun shines inside the bar. His thumb and forefinger open to a blank check. Left hand withdraws a Parker fountain pen from the other inside jacket pocket, unscrews the cap, places it between his fore-and middle fingers and then, right hand hovering, turns his face to mine.

"Can you have about twenty of these by this September? I'd like to publish."

It was April, the onset of spring.

"Of course. Definitely. Twenty Great Italians come September."

On the way out I said, "By the way, I would choose Yogi Berra."

It is difficult to put into words how I felt on the way back home that early spring day in the mid-1980s. Heart pounding. Terrified. The Dogwoods in the Village blossomed their pink flowers. I could smell the honeysuckle on the vines of my mother's front garden all the way from Brooklyn.

What did Shel do in town that spring and summer just before we met?

Once I had assayed into twenty Great Italians I made a copy at Eddie's xerox then carried the manuscript up to Max Zaz's office. He was not in. His wonderful wife was.

"I love my husband and don't want him to die," she was kind enough to share with me.

"I can help getting him to A.A.," I offered.

In the end, Zaz relied on his own resources to survive and flourish. Seriously ill in hospital, he gained his heath and later on, like Don Vincenzo, Barbra Williams and Bart Giamatti, he changed careers, from realizing the dreams of writers to providing succor to all those in need.

The phone rings. It's Max Zaz.

"We are going to publish your book. It is one of the best books America has ever produced. Oh, also, Tony, do you have time for a drink this Friday morning at the Gramercy Park Tavern? I'd like you to meet someone. Should say, someone wants to meet you. Another author of mine. Between you and me, as soon as I saw her author photo, I bought her book. Turned out it's very good, too. Eleven a.m. o.k.?"

Max and his other author, Barbra Williams, were already at the Tavern. I can see them now, sitting side by side at a far right, rear table, facing the entrance door. An empty booth awaited. I slid in face to face with Barbra and she started:

"I was telling Max how much I admire your writing. 'Nobody writes like Valerio anymore,' I told him."

"Well, thanks."

"She lives in Key West," Max mentioned.

Ernest Hemingway came to mind.

"Yes," she followed. "His house on Whitehead Street is near mine. And other fine writers are down there now. John Hersey, James Merrill, Joy Williams, Shel Silverstein, Phil Caputo. Of an evening, some of us meet at a bar squat on the Gulf."

I recall catching her soft dark eyes.

"You have to come down," she said to me.

In his wisdom, Max Zaz hit upon the idea of first option on my next book. First one Great Italian, then another.

"I want a monumental biography of Garibaldi and I am willing to pay you a respectable amount each month until that book is written and approved. Agreed?"

Piece-meal payments so that I could at least have one meal per day, utilities paid and a roof over my head. Life on the installment plan. Genius Max Zaz went on:

"Each month I will send you a certified check paid to your landlord plus utilities. And a modest separate check for recreational spending."

Few artists in Manhattan owned houses. Even Shel lived in a modest apartment.

"You have got to come down. You have got to come down" played like a mantra. One day after working on Max Zaz's monumental biography, I walked up to a travel agency in Rockefeller Center and purchased a one-way plane ticket J.F.K-Miami-Key West. I'd take Barbra Williams up on her invitation, and in Florida I would be closer to General Garibaldi's exploits in South America. Max Zaz did not have to know my exact movements. But my daughter Johanna did, and I phoned her.

"Sweetie, I'll be out of town for a while. Florida."

"How are you going?"

"Jet. Two-hour flight from J.F.K to Miami, then a DC-10 to Key West."

"You can't fly, dad."

"Sorry?"

"You can't fly. Yesterday we bombed Libya in retaliation for Muammar Gaddafi bombing a German discotheque American soldiers went to. Ten killed, 80 wounded. In retaliation we bombed him. They say we killed his daughter. There are going to be reprisals, dad. He bombs us, we bomb him, so on and so forth. You cannot fly now. Please."

I considered, Supposing I go ahead and fly in disregard of her presentiment of lethal danger, and her father's plane does go up in flames. She would be left with inconsolable sorrow, grave disappointment, and feel it was a damn shame because her father would still be alive if he had listened to her. She just was not important enough for him to listen.

"O.K.," I said. "I'll exchange my plane ticket for a train ticket. Thanks, Love."

I walked up to Pennsylvania Station, covering the same ground Shel and I covered on our way to his cigar maker, his typist's, and the Tenth Avenue Diner. Step up to an Amtrak ticket window.

"One-way ticket to Key West, please."

"Very well. Our special today, the Silver Streak, goes as far as Miami and includes a non-stop bus ticket to Key West. It's an overnight train."

"Ma'am, what is the cost of an upgrade to I think it's called a Roomette."

"This is your lucky day, sir. A free upgrade to a Roomette is available to you. Your Roomette will have all the accouterments of a small apartment. Stainless steel, pull out table/desk, curtains on the wall-to-wall window. An upper bunk."

A Roomette was definitely in Max Zaz's style.

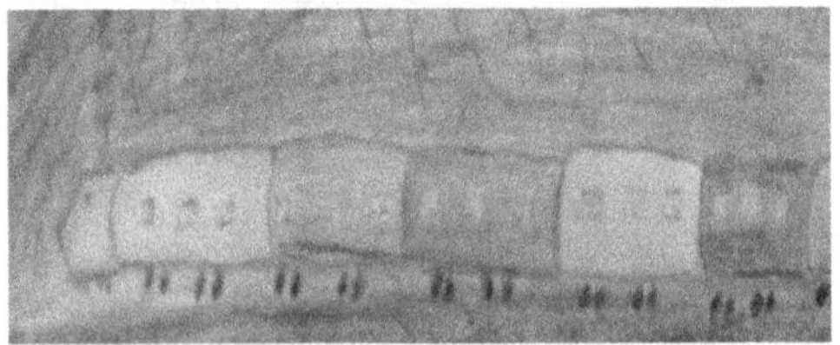

Trains, pencil drawing©Anthony Valerio20/20

"All aboard! Amtrak Silver Streak to Miami, Florida. Last call!"

Searching for Roomette #106. 112…1008….A conductor sidles up, holding a sheaf of papers with a picture I.D.

"Here it is, sir, your roomette. I'm your service captain, name's Vince. You have two locks, one outside here and one inside. I'll show you in."

He's wearing a maroon uniform with black buttons and a neat red cap with small peak.

"Here you go. Nice 'n cozy. Pull-out table can serve as a food and work space. You can step on this toilet top to reach your upper bunk. Any luggage, sir? I can hoist it up there for you."

" Just this shoulder bag. I have it. Thanks."

"Two calls for dinner. Seven and eight p.m. I can serve you in the dining car or here in your Roomette."

"Thank you."

Vince Patterson was a middle-aged black man, about five-nine, compact, very nice. His face, from a myriad of angles, especially his profile--he looked exactly like Louis Armstrong. The resemblance was astonishing. I took a chance.

"Vince, excuse me, but has anyone told you you look like Louie Armstrong?"

"Funny you should ask that because next month I'm going on a world tour singing Louie Armstrong's songs." And then there and then, in #106 Roomette on the Silver Streak, destination Miami, Florida, in 1987, he broke out into the Louis Armstrong favorite, "What a Wonderful World."

It was Louie Armstrong! Gravelly voice, musicianship, feel of the words to the music, unhurried.

"That's wonderful, Vince."

"Thanks. Oh, this switch here lights and alerts in my station any time of the day or night. First stop, Philadelphia."

Stretch out on the top bunk facing forward, the immediate future and unknown terrain just ahead. And then we pull out and in a flash that future recedes into the immediate past.

Philadelphia…Wilmington…. Place my face close up to my glass window and in the blackness of night outside take in a lit lamp post at the edge of a town, spotlighting ground that will forever go unnoticed. Washington D.C…. Through a thicket of trees a golf green emerges with unmoving flag. The temperature outside is heating up. Thoughts of my publisher's monumental biography filter in as the country speeds past. From the port of Marseilles, with a sentence of ignominious death hanging over his head in Italy, merchant captain Garibaldi bought the papers of a deceased seaman, took ship as second mate, and sailed to the port of Rio de Janeiro using a compass and guided by the stars. A few minutes after departing from Fredericksburg, Virginia, suddenly, the Silver Streak came to an abrupt halt. The lit face on my watch indicated 3:20 a.m. I ring for Vince. No response. Press my face harder against the glass. The more I looked into the total darkness, the more the vista came into view, dimly but tangible. An empty valley. Scan closer to the train. Crouched figures in silhouette were boarding, holding uzis. Nightmare? Not at all, because just then I hear my outer lock click open, turn toward the door, expecting to see Vince, and before I could hop down, my inside lock turns, slowly, deliberately, and in the middle of the night in the middle of nowhere the door to my Roomette opens, its light goes on and standing there looking at me, an open gold shield in his hand, is an athletic young man. He says:

“F.B.I. senior agent Ernie Grillo here. Do not panic. We would like to speak to you.”

Hop down and put on my pants. Hurriedly put on my shoes in the event I had to run. Here is exactly what Agent Grillo said next:

“Mr. Valerio, there is a bomb on this train. At present it is in a duffel bag at the feet of a passenger in an aisle seat in the car behind this one. A volunteer from the 80th training command center in Fredericksburg, J. Torres, noticed the rocket while walking up the aisle….” Grillo was holding a two-way radio. Copy this. Roger that. “It’s a highly flammable liquid fuel rocket, short, about two feet high. Officer Torres caught a glimpse of the nose cone. If that thing hits any surface and ignites, it can explode and blow two of these Amtrak cars to smithereens.”

“I saw—” pointing outside to the darkness.

“SWAT F.B.I. teams and two bomb-squad dogs have just boarded this train.”

“I didn’t see any dogs,” I said.

“You never do,” nonchalantly.

What happened was this:

Officer Jose Torres, on furlough to his home in Miami, in his first active combat duty jumped the perpetrator and hogtied his arms, legs and chest to the back of his seat.

"We are investigating the guy now," Grillo continued in my Roomette. "The bomb squad has diffused the rocket and is carrying it out to the empty field you can see in the near distance outside your window."

I said, "How do you know there are no other bombs on the train? Nobody checked my shoulder bag when I boarded."

"Exactly right. That's why we're searching all baggage right now. And here is where you come in."

"Me?"

"Yes. We have been watching you. You are cool as a cucumber, as they say, and you checked out. This train will make no further stops from here to Miami. We need you to lead the other passengers, especially the elderly, into the last two cars so that we can search the rest of the cars. Once you are all back there, make sure passengers remain calm, do not panic. Especially the elderly. Try to comfort them. We trust you to use your own words. There will be soft drinks, cakes, tea and coffee, even brandy."

"Yes, sir. One question. How did I check out?"

"Well, Mr. Valerio. When you throw out your garbage at your address in Greenwich Village, you do not tear up your phone bills. We were able to check all your outgoing and incoming phone calls of the past few months for anything, how can I say, suspicious, untoward. We found none."

"O. K. But I have someone waiting for me in Key West. God knows--"

"Here, use this radio. It's also a phone. Give a call."

I called Barbra Williams and woke her up close to the stars and told her not to be alarmed but there was a bomb on the train I was on coming to see her. Now all was under control. Barbra was happy I was safe and told me the next day she was scheduled to be at a function and then was going to Shel Silverstein's house. She would wait for me there. I remember feeling good that someone I hardly knew and someone I did not as yet know would worry on my behalf. Then I called Johanna and told her there was a bomb on the train but the situation was neutralized and her father and the other passengers were safe and I would call again once we arrived in Miami.

Straddling a gangway connection between two cars, keeping open the doors while passengers filed through, I directed--

"Let's go, everybody. Keep moving, please, into the last two cars. Nothing to be concerned about. We're just shifting cars for a bit. Shift happens. The situation is well under control. On your way now. Free refreshments ahead. Coffee, brandy, cake…."

We had our last coffee, Shel's and mine, in the springtime of 1998, at the Caffè Sha-Sha on Hudson Street. Seated at an outdoor table under a Cinzano umbrella.

"My son asked me to buy instruments for his band, " Shel said.

It was one of those moments in my time with Shel when I was rendered speechless. Here was a man who could outfit the finest symphony in the world with world class instruments, the violin section with Stradivari, and here he comes out with a declarative statement about his lone son's request for band instruments. Keyboard, guitar, bass, drums, maybe even a vibraphone, he would buy for his son and his band. Maybe as one of his song lyrics goes about a dad who did not leave his son or mom very much, Shel, a real father, would leave his son more than that. Fine instruments, he would leave his son and his band. And happy, he would make them.

"Oh, Shel, what happened to *Three Eyes*?"

"I decided to turn it into a play."

His thoughts fled to the new house he'd just bought on Martha's Vineyard.

"I can't get help to renovate it. No matter what I'm willing to pay, I can't get contractors out there." Then--"Anthony, I need recipes. My new place is far from a food mart. So I will be cooking a lot at home."

He raised his brows, smiling. In the end, Shel Silverstein was a man of few spoken words. He left openings for plying of the imagination. Mom Gertrude's kitchen in Brooklyn was narrow, with a four-burner stove, also pre-war. She's wearing a pretty lace-trimmed, blue blouse.

"Come, Shel," she says, "I'll show you how to make the meat sauce for your 'gourmet' dinner with my son, Anthony."

He sidles up to her.

"Here are the ingredients," she continues. "For your semolina you can use the Barilla brand. It's popular in Italy, too. One can use tomato paste. Fill the empty can with water. Onions. Load up on chopped onions. 2 cans Red Pack crushed tomatoes. Now for the meats. Shel, do you have a butcher near your house on the Vineyard? Failing that, a supermarket with a meat section?"

"I do not know but I will find out," he says.

"Here are the meats to use. Pork skin. Pork gives it the flavor. Roll up the skin and hold together with a toothpick. Beef tongue. Anthony was raised on animal innards, you know. Beef braciole. Meatballs. Before you add your meats, simmer your onions and tomato paste. About five, six minutes. Then add your meats. I place it all in this large stainless-steel skillet my father-in-law Don Antonio made for me. Then I let it simmer under a low flame throughout the night. Anthony likes this. He says the sweet aroma of my sauce permeates his sleep, his dreams."

"Garlic?" says Sheldon Allan.

"No. No garlic for this." And then she smiles and peers deeply into his eyes. "So it will leave your breath kissing sweet."

Back at the Café Sha-Sha, Shel says:

"She said she'd call me when she got to town. A blonde rollerblader from California. "

"Did she? Did she call you?" I asked.

"Not yet. But you should see her."

When it was time to go, I got up and beat him to the cash register. He rushes in.

"I got this one, Shel. It's O.K. You get the next big one."

Then we turned and looked out to Hudson Street. Hey, there she was! The blonde rollerblader from California. Skating in rhythm, pushing off the right skate, now the left, hands clasped behind her back. Advancing uptown, along with the traffic.

EPILOGUE

Shel's name remained on his downstairs bell for weeks after he died. Every time I passed on the way to watch the kids play ball, I stopped at his door where I had placed flowers on behalf of Barbra Williams and myself, and looked for his name on the tenant register. It was there. Time and time again on the way back home, I stood directly across the street from his place in front of St. Luke in the Fields church. Staring across at his second-storey window, I'd conjure him up, softly, to myself:

"Shel…."

Shel's Place

www.ingramcontent.com/pod-product-compliance
Lightning Source LLC
LaVergne TN
LVHW010626100826
845148LV00014B/3132

* 9 7 8 0 9 7 7 2 8 2 4 2 5 *